50 Cent
Hip-Hop Mogul
An Unauthorized Biography

D1413995

Jeff Burlingame

Speeding Star
Keep Boys Reading!

Library of Congress Cataloging-in-Publication Data

Burlingame, Jeff, author.
  50 Cent : hip-hop mogul / Jeff Burlingame.
    pages cm. — (Hip-hop moguls)
  Includes bibliographical references and index.
  Summary: "In this biography of Hip-Hop mogul 50 Cent, learn about the struggles the star
    went through, including selling crack cocaine and being shot nine times"—Provided by
    publisher.
  ISBN 978-1-62285-201-7
  1. 50 Cent (Musician)—Juvenile literature. 2. Rap musicians—United States—Biography—
    Juvenile literature. I. Title.
  ML3930.A13B87 2014
  782.421649'092—dc23
  [B]   2013044935

Future Editions:
Paperback ISBN: 978-1-62285-202-4   EPUB ISBN: 978-1-62285-203-1
Single-User PDF ISBN: 978-1-62285-204-8   Multi-User PDF: 978-1-62285-205-5

Printed in the United States of America
052014 Lake Book Manufacturing, Inc., Melrose Park, IL
10 9 8 7 6 5 4 3 2 1

This book has not been authorized by 50 Cent or his agents.

To Our Readers:

We have done our best to make sure all Internet addresses in this book were active and appropriate when we went to press. However, the author and the Publisher have no control over, and assume no liability for, the material available on those Internet sites or on other Web sites they may link to. Any comments or suggestions can be sent by e-mail to comments@speedingstar.com or to the address below:

Speeding Star
Box 398, 40 Industrial Road
Berkeley Heights, NJ 07922
USA
www.speedingstar.com

✪ Enslow Publishers, Inc., is committed to printing our books on recycled paper. The paper in every book contains 10% to 30% post-consumer waste (PCW). The cover board on the outside of each book contains 100% PCW. Our goal is to do our part to help young people and the environment too!

Illustration Credits: ©AP Images/Amy Sussman/Invision for Feeding America, p. 37; ©AP Images/Anthony Behar/Sipa USA, p. 42; ©AP Images/Bebeto Matthews, p. 30; ©AP Images/Bob Child, p. 13; ©AP Images/Boris Grdanoski, p. 44; ©AP Images/Chris Carlson, p. 35; ©AP Images/Chris Pizzello, p. 23; ©AP Images/Eric Jamison, p. 17; ©AP Images/Erik S. Lesser, p. 10; ©AP Images/Jason DeCrow, p. 19; ©AP Images/Jim Cooper, p. 6; ©AP Images/Kevork Djansezian, pp. 9, 15; ©AP Images/Krista Niles, p. 22; ©AP Images/Mark J. Terrill, p. 36; ©AP Images/Matt Sayles, pp. 4, 38; ©AP Images/Peter Kramer, p. 8; ©AP Images/Ramin Talaie, p. 28; ©AP Images/Seth Wenig, p. 29.

Cover Illustration: ©AP Images/Matt Sayles

Contents

With three songs recently released to the radio and an upcoming deal with a major record label, 50 Cent was a rising rap star with a lot to lose as he sat in a car outside of his grandmother's house in Queens, New York late one Wednesday morning in May 2000.

It is then the twenty-four-year-old musician's dreams—not to mention his life—nearly ended. Seemingly out of nowhere, a man jumped out of the passenger seat of another vehicle, ran up to 50 Cent's car, and

chapter 1

Shot and Dropped

After fully recovering from being shot nine times, 50 Cent is shown in 2003 wearing a bulletproof vest.

began shooting his 9MM pistol into it. Nine bullets hit various parts of 50 Cent's body. The bullets shattered his bones, and one of them exploded through the side of his face, blowing a hole in his jaw and embedding shrapnel in his tongue.

"I was scared the whole time," 50 Cent told MTV a few years after the shooting. "Ain't nobody gonna tell you they ain't scared in that situation. It's a hit, man. You supposed to die in that situation…. I was looking in the rearview mirror like, 'Oh, [expletive], somebody shot me in the face! It burns. Burns, burns, burns."

50 Cent's young son was inside the home and heard the gunshots. His great-grandmother phoned for help. Her grandson was rushed to the hospital and spent several hours in surgery while doctors removed bullets from his body. He spent thirteen days in the hospital. He spent several months after his release recovering from his wounds.

On the first day he was in the hospital, 50 Cent signed the paperwork on his music deal with Columbia Records. He knew if word of his being shot got back to the company, it might withdraw the offer. No company wanted to deal with a client who was going to be a headache. And being involved in a lifestyle that would lead one to get shot nine times certainly qualified one as a headache. 50 Cent knew this, so he had his grandmother bring him the documents for him to sign. His speedy signing turned out to be a smart move.

7

"As soon as word got out that I'd been shot, all my calls started going directly to people's voicemails," 50 Cent wrote in his 2007 book, *50 X 50: 50 Cent in His Own Words*. "None of the people would call me back either. It didn't take too long for me to figure out where I stood with them. I knew it was only a matter of time before they dropped me."

Three days after he was shot, 50 Cent was scheduled to film a music video for one of his singles, "Thug Love."

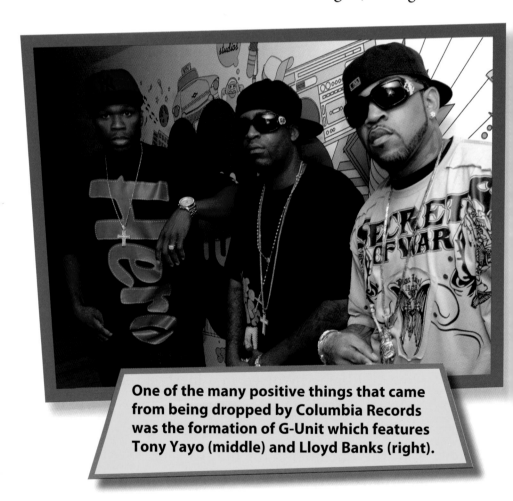

One of the many positive things that came from being dropped by Columbia Records was the formation of G-Unit which features Tony Yayo (middle) and Lloyd Banks (right).

Even though he had to take a step backward early in his career, 50 Cent found his way to the top of the rap/hip-hop world.

The video, like the song, was to feature popular all-female singing group, Destiny's Child. Releasing the video easily could have been the move that made him a household name. Of course, the video shoot didn't happen. 50 Cent's first major-label record, *Power of the Dollar*, also didn't happen because of the shooting. *Power of the Dollar* was scheduled to be released in July by Columbia Records. But the company decided to drop 50 Cent from its roster, just as the rapper feared it would.

9

50 Cent's career dreams appeared to be as traumatized as his body.

"There was no Plan B for me," he told *AOL Music* in 2003. "If I don't make music, I'm going back to the hood. I'll sell crack. I'm gonna go back to sell crack if I can't make it in the music business and that's because that's what I was doing before that…. I make music cuz it's almost like I can escape everything I was involved in."

One of 50 Cent's biggest supporters is Russell Simmons who also is considered a hip-hop mogul.

Everything 50 Cent had been involved in before he began performing music read like the sad script to a tragic play. As he said, there were drugs. There also were murders, orphanhood, poverty, jail cells, and stabbings. Before music, little about 50 Cent's life had been what one might consider a success.

Now, after the shooting, it appeared he was heading right back where he came from. He wrote in *50 X 50*, "Here I had spent the last three years putting all my time and money into music, trying to leave the street behind me, and it was the street that was gonna stop me from finding success. ...I was lying there all [messed] up, not knowing how my voice was gonna sound, whether or not I was gonna be able to walk right again. ...That was the only time during the whole period that I cried—I truly felt in my heart that my music career was over."

Somehow, 50 Cent remained optimistic that he still could make it—both in the music industry and in life in general. He told *AOL Music*, "You get shot nine times you feel like you here for a reason, 'specially when the guy shooting you is [right next to you]. ... [Y]ou gotta feel God made the shells land where they land."

Despite it all, 50 Cent didn't give up on his dreams. Instead, he simply took a step backward. He returned to the streets, but this time it was with music on his mind. He had overcome too much adversity in his life to allow anything—even a near-fatal shooting—to stop him now.

11

From the beginning, it was evident life was not going to be easy for 50 Cent, who was born Curtis James Jackson III on July 6, 1975, in the South Jamaica neighborhood in the New York City borough of Queens. Curtis was named after his grandfather who, along with his grandmother, Beulah, played the most pivotal roles in his rearing. That is because his mother, Sabrina Jackson, was a hustler who often could be found on the streets doing whatever it took to make money for herself and

Chapter 2

Street Hustler

her child, including selling drugs. She was only fifteen years old when Curtis was born. No one knew who Curtis's father was.

"My mother never told me who my father was," 50 Cent wrote years later in his book, *50 X 50*, "and I don't even know that she knew. I remember being with her in the park one time—I had to have been about four years old—and I saw all the other kids playing with their dads. I asked her where my daddy was. She told me that I had been born through Immaculate Conception, that she was both my mom and my dad."

Even though 50 wasn't a fan of school, he now realizes the importance of an education. That is why he visits schools; to push children to stay in school.

Until he was eight years old, Curtis was shuffled between his grandparents' house in Queens and his mother's apartment on Long Island. It was in that apartment that, in 1983, his mother was murdered. Someone had knocked her unconscious, turned on the gas, and left her there to die. Curtis then went to live with his grandparents for good. He told MTV years later, "My grandmother and them told me, 'Your mother's not coming home. She's not gonna come back to pick you up. You're gonna stay with us now.'"

Curtis moved into the cramped two-story home along with his grandparents and several aunts and uncles. On Sundays, the large family would dress up in their best clothes and head off to the local Baptist church. In school, Curtis was a hyper kid who found it difficult to sit still for lessons. For a period of time, his grandmother even tried treating his hyperactivity with medicine.

When he hit junior high school, Curtis suddenly became less interested in school. Now twelve years old, he began hustling the streets, just as his mother had done when she was only a little older than he was then. For Curtis, street hustling also meant selling drugs. It was money that drew him to that lifestyle. The money Curtis's grandfather made at his job working on cars was enough to cover the basic bills for his large family, but it was not enough to purchase anything extravagant. Curtis wanted extravagance. He had been raised in an environment where drugs were commonplace, so that made his decision an easy one.

Hip-hop artist 50 Cent reacts as he accepts the award for best new artist during the 3rd annual BET Awards, Tuesday, June 24, 2003, in Los Angeles—a scene far removed from his early life on the streets.

"It started for me because I would always be asking my mother's old friends for new sneakers and things like that," he wrote in *50 X 50*. "At first they felt bad for me and would take me to the shoe store to get me a new pair or whatever. ...By the time I got to be twelve, it was counterproductive for them to keep doing that, so they started giving me bags of dope so I could provide for myself."

For years, Curtis lived a double life. At home, he acted like the proper grandson he always had been. Outside his grandparents' house, he was earning a reputation as a top-level hustler, making just enough cash to buy fancy clothes but not enough for cars or other more costly goods. Each day, he would head off for school and then cut class, taking to the streets to sell rocks of crack cocaine. Then he would return home as if nothing wrong had happened, hiding the drugs from his grandparents.

One morning, however, his lifestyle caught up with him. The night before, he had hidden the crack he was selling in a pair of shoes. The next day, he carried those shoes to school and a teacher found the drugs inside them. Curtis was arrested and given probation. He wrote in *50 X 50*: "[I]t meant that I had to change schools and go from Andrew Jackson to Martin Van Buren, which was the last straw for me. After that, I didn't really care about school. ...Hustling became my entire focus."

The sport of boxing was the only thing that took the teenager off the streets. The slightly pudgy kid

50 Cent used to work closely with boxer Floyd Mayweather Jr., before starting his own company, called SMS Promotions. From left to right, he is shown with Justin Bieber, Lil Wayne, Mayweather, and Yuriorkis Gamboa.

would spend hours each day after school in a sweaty gym sparring with other kids and learning the craft. He became good at it too, and eventually competed in the Junior Olympics. But Curtis's life on the streets eventually delivered a technical knockout to his life in the ring, and he quit boxing for good. To defend himself on the streets, he decided he needed something bigger than his fists and started carrying a gun.

By the time he was nineteen years old, Curtis Jackson III had been arrested several times, including

one time where he was sentenced to a lengthy drug-rehab program. He told the judge at the time, he didn't use drugs and never had. He only sold them. He earned his General Equivalency Diploma [GED] when he was in the program. But instead of using that GED to get him into college or a job after he was released, he headed back to the streets.

He told *The Guardian* in 2003, "Someone says to you, if you stay in school, in eight years you can have a new car. And the kid looks round his neighborhood and sees someone who got [the car] in six months. Hustling doesn't seem like one of the options, it seems like the only option."

Curtis Jackson III returned to street hustling, but soon realized he needed to change his ways following his nearly two-year stint in the drug-rehab program. To begin that change, he decided he needed a new name. His close friends and family knew him as "Boo-Boo," but that nickname certainly wasn't one that would earn him any street credibility. So he chose to call himself "50 Cent." Over the years, Jackson has given two different explanations as to why he chose the nickname. The first,

Chapter 3

A New Name

Starting out with a reputation as just a talented rapper, 50 Cent also became known for always giving back. He is shown performing at "A Night for Vets: An MTV Concert for the BRAVE."

he told *Time* magazine, was because "[I]t was a metaphor for change." The second, he said on several occasions, was in honor of a New York City robber named Kelvin Martin, whose nickname had been "50 Cent." Whatever the real reason, the nickname stuck. Forever more, he would be known as 50 Cent, or sometimes "Fiddy," "Fifty," or "50."

50 Cent started working out religiously after his release from rehab, and he also began to mess around with rap music. He soon gained a reputation as a talented rapper, performing his street-influenced, drawling rhymes at parties and other small-time social gatherings. He enjoyed rapping, but it didn't appear his talent for the craft was going to take him anywhere. That is until around the time of his twenty-first birthday.

That year, 1996, 50 Cent was introduced to Jason Mizell, aka Jam Master Jay, the DJ for the groundbreaking hip-hop group Run-D.M.C. A decade earlier, Run-D.M.C. had been the most successful rap group in the world. When 50 Cent met him, Jam Master Jay was running his own record label and signing and developing talent for it. Jam Master Jay saw something he liked in 50 Cent, and agreed to help him, too. He taught 50 Cent a lot not only about the music industry, but also about music itself.

"[H]e taught me about song format," 50 Cent told *AOL Music*. "I didn't even know how to count bars till I got around Jam Master Jay."

Jam Master Jay is one of the biggest reasons that 50 is where he is today. Unfortunately, Jam Master Jay lost his life during a recording session at his studio on October 30, 2002.

Jam Master Jay eventually signed his protégé to his record label, Jam Master Jay Records. He took 50 Cent into a music studio for the first time and let him rap on a single from a group he was producing named Onyx. Jay and 50 Cent worked together for a couple years. "I had recorded over an album's worth of material while I was under Jam Master Jay," 50 Cent told *Billboard* magazine in 2003. "[But] his touring schedule with Run-DMC had become so hectic that he wasn't able to focus on me at the time, so I moved on."

The aspiring rapper's personal life was hectic at the time, as well. He was now a father. On October 13, 1997, his girlfriend, Shaniqua Tompkins, had given birth to a boy the young couple named Marquise. His son's birth, 50 Cent told *The Independent* in 2004, marked the beginning of the end for his hustling ways: "Going to jail in those days wasn't much of a deal, because I had no one to take care of but myself. My little boy changed everything."

The songs 50 Cent had recorded with Jam Master Jay soon helped get him noticed by other producers. Among those producers were two men who called themselves the Trackmasters. The Trackmasters—Jean-Claude "Poke" Olivier and Samuel "Tone" Barnes—were well known in the rap industry. They had produced

The song "How to Rob" can be viewed as a stepping stone for 50 Cent when it comes to stirring up problems. 50 performs with former G-Unit member The Game (left).

23

hit records for all the era's top hip-hop stars, including Nas, R. Kelly, and Jay-Z. The Trackmasters liked what they heard from 50 Cent, and decided to help get him signed to Columbia Records. The label sent the aspiring rapper to a New York studio, where he recorded dozens of songs that were to be the basis for his debut album, *Power of the Dollar.*

The forthcoming album's debut single, "How to Rob," featured 50 Cent rapping about how he was going to rob several of the days' most popular entertainers. Those entertainers included Jay-Z, actor Will Smith, and boxer Mike Tyson. The song was included on the soundtrack to the movie *In Too Deep*, and was praised by the few critics who bothered to review it. Those who were listed as robbing victims on the song, however, did not like it. Some even fired back at 50 Cent in their own songs. Most wondered who he was because they had never heard of him. 50 Cent said the song was intended to be a joke, but also that there was some seriousness to it, too. He told *Rolling Stone* magazine, "When robbery's not out of the question, it's kinda easy for a song like that to fall into your thought pattern. Bigger artists have bigger diamonds. Kids in the hood is looking at the TV, going, 'Damn it, look at that [stuff] he got on!' Rappers have egos, so I was anticipating them being upset. But I didn't care, 'cause it had been a year since the deal with Columbia, and I'm still selling crack."

The publicity for "How to Rob" helped the song crack the top 100 songs on *Billboard*'s Hot R&B/Hip-

Hop chart. 50 Cent's second single, "Rowdy Rowdy," did not make any of *Billboard*'s charts, and neither did his third release, "Thug Love," which featured a chorus sung by Destiny's Child.

But 50 Cent still had momentum and had built a bit of a name for himself. He had three singles under his belt, and a major-label deal with Columbia Records waiting to be signed. It seemed as if he had the world at his fingertips. But the nine bullet wounds he received while seated in a car in the front of his grandparents' house in Queens on May 24, 2000 derailed his opportunity. It sent him to the hospital, ruined his deal with Columbia, and left him at the lowest point in his life that had been filled with low points.

One of those low points had come two months prior to the shooting, when 50 Cent was stabbed by those associated with a rival hip-hop group outside a New York recording studio. The incident was believed to be related to 50 Cent's longtime rivalry with a rapper from Queens named Ja Rule. The shooting incident, 50 Cent said, made him reevaluate his life.

"Being shot isn't as bad as not knowing what you are going to do with your life," he told *The Independent.* "If you send a person back to where I'm from with no direction, then you sentence them to death or to killing somebody. He's gonna be involved in something he ain't supposed to be involved in."

No longer with a record deal, 50 Cent began recording songs on his own and selling them as mixtapes—

25

underground recordings released independently of a record label. Those mixtapes resulted in a huge buzz and the eventual release of the album *Guess Who's Back?* The album eventually hit number 28 on *Billboard*'s top 200 chart and sold nearly a half-million copies.

By that time, 2002, twenty-seven-year-old 50 Cent had connected with several business and musical partners, including Lloyd Banks and Tony Yayo, with whom he formed the hip-hop group G-Unit. The smooth-flowing 50 Cent was becoming well-known in hip-hop circles, and the biggest break of his career was just around the corner.

A copy of one of 50 Cent's mixtapes that made its way to rapper Eminem started a chain of events that eventually would make the Queens-raised musician a household name. When he first heard 50 Cent's music in 2002, Marshall "Eminem" Mathers was a music-industry mogul who had sold millions of records as a rapper and had founded a record label that sold millions more records.

Eminem fell in love with 50 Cent's authentic, gangster lyrics. Eminem,

Chapter 4

"Something About 50"

After his mixtapes became instant hits, Eminem and Dr. Dre did all they could to sign 50 Cent. After a long wait, they were able to sign him to a joint deal between Aftermath Records and Shady Records.

along with his partner, the legendary musician Dr. Dre, immediately attempted to sign 50 Cent to a recording contract. But Eminem and Dr. Dre weren't the only ones trying to do so. The success of his mixtapes had made 50 Cent a hot commodity in the world of hip-hop, and other labels had been soliciting his services, as well.

Eminem and Dr. Dre flew 50 Cent out to Los Angeles to meet with them. Eminem believed 50 Cent was the real deal. He was not a phony. He had lived through all the dire situations he was rapping about. He had been stabbed. He had been shot. He had shot and stabbed others. He had even been accused of at least one killing, that of his former mentor Jam Master Jay, who was shot to death in his recording studio on October 30, 2002. 50 Cent repeatedly denied any involvement in the murder.

"His life story sold me," Eminem told *XXL* magazine in 2003. "To have a story behind the music

After his immediate success in the rap/hip-hop world, 50 Cent decided to venture into other markets. He launched a clothing line called the G-Unit Clothing Company that he regularly sports.

After starring in the film *Get Rich or Die Tryin'*, 50 Cent published his first book entitled *From Pieces to Weight: Once Upon a Time in Southside Queens.*

is so important. He's just got the total package. He can write songs—not just freestyle. He picks good beats and writes good hooks. But there is something about 50 as an MC."

Eminem and Dr. Dre won over 50 Cent, as well, and signed him to a million-dollar contract. They soon released a few of his songs on the soundtrack for the movie about Eminem's life called *8 Mile*. One of those songs, "Wanksta," was released as a single and rose to number thirteen on *Billboard*'s singles chart. The anticipation was building for 50 Cent's first album with Eminem and Dr. Dre.

That album, *Get Rich or Die Tryin'*, was released in February 2003. It was an immediate success, selling nearly one million copies the first week it was available. That was a record for a debut artist. By the end of the year, the album had sold 6 million copies. Sparked by the number-one lead single "In Da Club," *Get Rich or Die Tryin'* was a crossover success, enjoyed not only by fans of hip-hop but also by fans of pop music. In *50 X 50*, Fiddy wrote: "It was crazy. In cities all over the country my record sold out. As in, there was not a single store in that entire city where you could find my record. Everywhere I went, I was mobbed. I literally could not go more than a few minutes without hearing my single, 'In Da Club,' coming from a radio or car stereo."

The people controlling those radios or car stereos weren't the only ones who liked 50 Cent's album. Critics raved about it, too, and so did fellow rappers.

Superstar rapper and producer Sean "P. Diddy" Combs told MTV, "I love the 50 Cent album. I've never really felt anticipation on an artist like that and I've dealt with Biggie [Smalls] and watched Dr. Dre and Snoop [Dogg]. This is a new type of beast." That beast, 50 Cent, received five Grammy Award nominations in 2004, including Best New Artist and Best Rap Album.

Like many successful hip-hop artists before him, 50 Cent expanded upon his musical success with a line of other ventures. He created G-Unit Clothing Line, and began acting, starring in a film about his life, *Get Rich or Die Tryin'*, named after his recent hit album. He also wrote an autobiography titled *From Pieces to Weight: Once Upon a Time in Southside Queens*. Then he founded his own record label, G-Unit Records.

None of the other ventures he was involved in took 50 Cent away from his music career for long. In March 2005, his second album, *The Massacre*, was released. The release—featuring the singles "Disco Inferno," "Candy Shop," and "Just a Lil Bit"—debuted at number one on *Billboard*'s chart and sold more than one million copies in its first week.

Overall, critics gave the album slightly worse reviews than they had for 50 Cent's previous release. By no means was that a knock on *The Massacre*, however. It was simply a nod to the fact that 50 Cent's first album had been considered an all-time classic. *The Massacre*'s cover, similar to the cover of *Get Rich or Die Tryin'*,

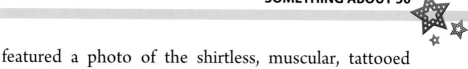

featured a photo of the shirtless, muscular, tattooed artist whose music was featured inside.

Yet, although he was no longer selling drugs, 50 still got wrapped up in his share of mischief. On New Year's Day 2003, for example, just before he signed his record deal with Eminem and Dr. Dre, 50 Cent and four other men were arrested when police found two loaded guns in the car they were in. At various times, 50 Cent has justified his carrying of guns to the media. He said he's concerned for his safety. He wears a bulletproof vest and bulletproofs all his cars. "Some places, they have next to no gun violence," he told *The Independent*. "We have a lot of gun violence. Where I'm from, you can be a victim or an aggressor. In some situations those are the only options."

In 2004, 50 Cent was arrested for assault and battery when he jumped into the crowd during one of his concerts in Massachusetts and allegedly punched a woman in the face. Then, in 2006, he was pulled over for weaving his silver Lamborghini in and out of traffic in New York. As Eminem said: 50 Cent wasn't faking the adverse situations and ghetto lifestyle he was rapping about. He was living it—both before and after he became successful.

Spectacle surrounded the release of 50 Cent's third album, *Curtis*, in 2007. The show began months earlier, when it was determined that 50 Cent's new album was going to be released the same day, September 11, as Kanye West's new album. There was no disputing that the two men were the hottest hip-hop artists in the world. But which one was the best? Fans believed September 11 would provide the answer. Whichever artist's record sold the most clearly would be the most popular.

Chapter 5

Sales Showdown

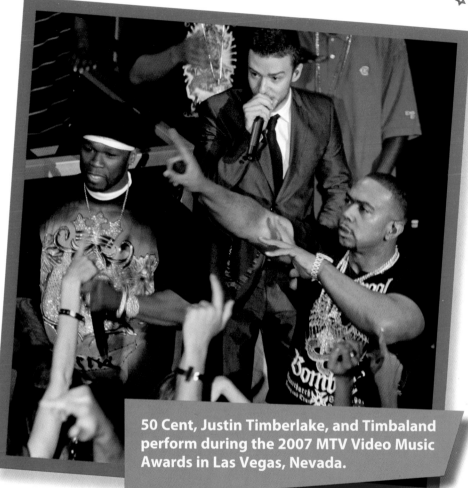

50 Cent, Justin Timberlake, and Timbaland perform during the 2007 MTV Video Music Awards in Las Vegas, Nevada.

Members of the media ran with the battle, hyping it in their stories in newspapers, magazines, and online. 50 Cent told *Time* magazine what fans should expect from the new album: "You should expect a lot of surprises. For my last two albums, I isolated myself to working with only members of G-Unit [50 Cent's original rap group]. On this album I worked with Justin Timberlake, Robin Thicke, Mary J. Blige, Akon, Nicole [Scherzinger] from the Pussycat Dolls, Dr. Dre, and Eminem. I'm in a place where I'm secure enough to have all these other talented people around me because I've proven myself, with my first two projects selling over 21 million copies."

Both 50 Cent and Kanye West played up their competition. But 50 Cent soon took it to another level. In an August interview with the Web site *SOHH.com*,

With all of the hype going on between both artist's soon-to-be released albums, 50 Cent and Kanye West were trying to "fuel the fire" by presenting an award together at the 2007 MTV Video Music Awards, just two days before the release of both albums.

In 2012, 50 Cent joined up with Feeding America and the Food Bank for New York City to help serve Thanksgiving meals to those who were affected by Hurricane Sandy.

he said he was willing to pay the ultimate price if his album sold fewer copies than Kanye's. He said, "If Kanye West sells more records than 50 Cent on September 11, I'll no longer write music. I'll write music and work with my other artists, but I won't put out anymore solo albums."

50 Cent later said he had made that promise only to stoke the fire and help sell more albums. It was a good

thing he thought he was joking. During the first week of its release, *Curtis* sold 691,000 copies. Meanwhile, Kanye's album, *Graduation*, sold 957,000 copies during the same period. Part of the reason he lost the competition, 50 Cent believed, was because the video for one of the songs, "Follow My Lead," had been leaked on the Internet a month before the release of *Curtis*. The leak angered 50 Cent so much that he ripped a television off the wall in his office and threw his cellphone through an unopened window.

Fifty's showing may have been disappointing to him, but it was one most artists would have died for.

50 Cent and Justin Timberlake are shown on stage together at the Justin Timberlake and Friends concert which benefited Shriners Hospitals for Children.

Curtis only reached number two on the Billboard album charts in the United States, but it was number one in several other countries, including Australia, Ireland, and Switzerland. In general, critics did not like 50 Cent's new album as much as they had his previous two. The lukewarm reception of his new album did little to hurt 50 Cent's bottom line. *Forbes* magazine said he was the second-wealthiest hip-hop artist in 2007, and that he had made $32 million the previous year. The following year, the magazine said, he made $150 million.

The rapper told *ABC News* in 2009, that no matter how much money he had he always wanted more. He said, "I think ambition is leading me through an endless tunnel. You know, I think there won't be a point that I'm completely satisfied. I meet people that are wealthy while I may be what they consider rich…. Wealth is a lot more. I think I'm rich because I'm around people that have a few billion dollars. So it sends me back to a space where I'm ready to hustle and get it going and do more."

50 Cent donated some of that money to charities. Most notable among those was the G-Unity Foundation, which 50 Cent created to help serve children and others living in urban communities such as the area of Queens he was raised in. A large portion of 50 Cent's money could have gone to the mother of his son, had she won a court case she filed in 2008. Shaniqua Tompkins sued the rapper for $50 million, saying that he had promised to take care of her for life if he became a star. The lawsuit eventually was dismissed, but 50 Cent said his ex was

bitter and would not let him see his Marquise, then eleven years old, as much as he had been.

The album 50 Cent initially had planned to release in 2007 instead of *Curtis* finally was released two years later. Titled *Before I Self Destruct*, the album's songs featured some of the heaviest beats 50 Cent had rapped over in years. Critics said *Before I Self Destruct* was 50 Cent returning to the harder-edge style he had portrayed on his earlier albums. But, unfortunately for the rapper, his fans didn't turn out to buy the record in as large of numbers as they had those earlier releases. Only 160,000 people purchased *Before I Self Destruct* in the first week it was on the market.

For his part, 50 Cent blamed the poor sales on a leak of the album that had occurred weeks before it was officially released in November 2009. "For myself, I'm asking myself, 'What did you expect, bro? Your fans got it when it was available, at the first available opportunity,'" he said on Sirius Satellite Radio. "For me this album is a prequel—it's full circle. When the energy around a project is the way this is, you can't really feel like it's a failure."

The relatively poor showing of *Before I Self Destruct* came during a down period in 50 Cent's life, a time where he said he lost several million dollars in the stock market during America's Great Recession. He even had to put his nineteen-bedroom, thirty-seven-bathroom Connecticut mansion—once owned by boxer Mike Tyson—up for sale.

The release of *Before I Self Destruct* marked the beginning of the driest spell of 50 Cent's decade-long recording career. He did release some individual songs—most notably "Crack A Bottle" with Eminem, which won a coveted Grammy Award. But as far as entire albums were concerned, 50 Cent appeared to no longer be in the game.

"There was finance stuff that gave me writer's block," he told *Vanity Fair* in 2013. "Then it came together. Everything is fine

Chapter 6

Still Searching

In October 2013, 50 Cent appeared at the New York City premiere for the film *Escape Plan* in which he stars as the character Hush.

now. It kind of helped, though. It gave me a chance to take a step back and enjoy it from fans' perspective. Because when you're in it, you're in it."

The rapper will reportedly get back "in it" in 2014 with the release of his fifth and sixth studio albums, *Animal Ambition* and *Street King Immortal*. The latter originally was scheduled to be released earlier, but kept getting delayed for various reasons.

As his fans waited for the release of *Street King Immortal*, 50 Cent kept his name in the headlines. The biggest news surrounding him was not positive. In June 2013, 50 Cent was charged with domestic violence for allegedly kicking model Daphne Joy and causing damage to her California condo. At the time, Daphne Joy and 50 Cent had dated for three years. During her relationship with 50 Cent, Daphne Joy gave birth to a boy, 50 Cent's son Sire Jackson.

On Monday, October 28, 2013, 50 Cent's attorney, Scott Leemon, shared this statement: "Curtis '50 Cent' Jackson has entered into an agreement with the Los Angeles City Attorney to resolve the charges against him. The agreement called for Mr. Jackson to plead no contest to a single count of misdemeanor vandalism; which deals with the door of the apartment that was damaged and owned by the landlord. All remaining counts, including, the domestic violence charge will be dismissed. He has agreed to perform community service, attend counseling sessions and will be on unsupervised probation for a period of three (3) years."

50 Cent once told *Rolling Stone* magazine. "With some artists, people look at them and wanna be that artist," "I don't think people wanna be me. I'm still searching for my purpose. I do have defects of character. When I get mad, I get mad. I can do things and say things that aren't nice. And people, they look at me and they go, 'Well, he's crazy.' Is crazy bad? Me being crazy is ... I'm all right with that."

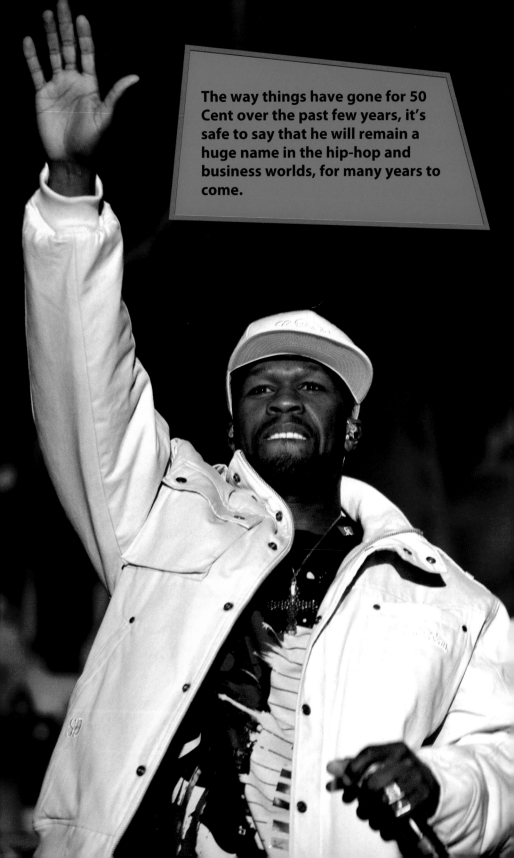

The way things have gone for 50 Cent over the past few years, it's safe to say that he will remain a huge name in the hip-hop and business worlds, for many years to come.

Discography

Get Rich or Die Tryin', 2004

The Massacre, 2005

Curtis, 2007

Before I Self Destruct, 2007

Street King Immortal, 2014?

Animal Ambition, 2014?

Internet Addresses

OFFICIAL WEB SITE
www.50cent.com
OFFICIAL TWITTER PAGE
www.twitter.com/50cent

Selected Honors and Awards

2003 Favorite Rap/Hip-Hop Male Artist, American Music Awards

Favorite Rap/Hip-Hop Album, American Music Awards

Best New Artist, BET Awards

Best Male Hip-Hop Artist, BET Awards

Rap Artist of the Year, *Billboard* Music Awards

R&B Artist of the Year, *Billboard* Music Awards

Artist of the Year, *Billboard* Music Awards

Best New Artist, MTV Video Music Awards

Best Rap Video, MTV Video Music Awards

Album of the Year, *Source* Awards

Breakthrough Artist of the Year, *Source* Awards

Single of the Year, Male, *Source* Awards

Best Artist 2003, World Music Awards

Best New Artist, World Music Awards

Best Pop Male Artist, World Music Awards

Best Rap/Hip-Hop Artist, World Music Awards

Best R&B Artist, World Music Awards

2005   Favorite Rap/Hip-Hop Album, American Music Awards

Artist of the Year, *Billboard* Music Awards

Album of the Year, *Billboard* Music Awards

Hot 100 Artist of the Year, *Billboard* Music Awards

Rap Artist of the Year, *Billboard* Music Awards

R&B/Hip-Hop Artist of the Year, *Billboard* Music Awards

Ringtone of the Year, *Billboard* Music Awards

Top Rap Albums, *Billboard* R&B/Hip-Hop Awards

Top R&B/Hip-Hop Album Artist, *Billboard* R&B/Hip-Hop Awards

Top R&B/Hip-Hop Albums, *Billboard* R&B/Hip-Hop Awards

World's Best Selling Rap/Hip-Hop Artist, World Music Awards

2006   Best Hip-Hop Video, MTV Video Music Awards Japan

2007   World's Best Selling Rap/Hip-Hop Artist, World Music Awards

2010   Best Rap Performance by a Duo or Group, Grammy Awards(With Eminem and Dr. Dre)

Index